SUPER CUTE!

Baby Rabbits

by Bethany Olson

BLASTOFF! READERS

BELLWETHER MEDIA · MINNEAPOLIS, MN

Note to Librarians, Teachers, and Parents:

Blastoff! Readers are carefully developed by literacy experts and combine standards-based content with developmentally appropriate text.

Level 1 provides the most support through repetition of high-frequency words, light text, predictable sentence patterns, and strong visual support.

Level 2 offers early readers a bit more challenge through varied simple sentences, increased text load, and less repetition of high-frequency words.

Level 3 advances early-fluent readers toward fluency through increased text and concept load, less reliance on visuals, longer sentences, and more literary language.

Level 4 builds reading stamina by providing more text per page, increased use of punctuation, greater variation in sentence patterns, and increasingly challenging vocabulary.

Level 5 encourages children to move from "learning to read" to "reading to learn" by providing even more text, varied writing styles, and less familiar topics.

Whichever book is right for your reader, Blastoff! Readers are the perfect books to build confidence and encourage a love of reading that will last a lifetime!

This edition first published in 2014 by Bellwether Media, Inc.

No part of this publication may be reproduced in whole or in part without written permission of the publisher. For information regarding permission, write to Bellwether Media, Inc., Attention: Permissions Department, 5357 Penn Avenue South, Minneapolis, MN 55419.

Library of Congress Cataloging-in-Publication Data

Olson, Bethany.
 Baby rabbits / by Bethany Olson.
   p. cm. – (Blastoff! readers. Super cute!)
 Audience: K to grade 3.
 Summary: "Developed by literacy experts for students in kindergarten through grade three, this book introduces baby rabbits to young readers through leveled text and related photos"– Provided by publisher.
 Includes bibliographical references and index.
 ISBN 978-1-60014-932-0 (hardcover : alk. paper)
 1. Rabbits–Infancy–Juvenile literature. I. Title.
 SF453.2.O47 2014
 599.32'139–dc23
                                                    2013008243

Printed in the United States of America, North Mankato, MN.

Table of Contents

Kits!

Baby rabbits are called kits. Some live in the wild. Others are **pets**.

Life in the Litter

Kits are born in **litters**. One litter can have more than ten kits.

Young kits live in
a nest or **burrow**.
They cuddle close
to stay warm.

Mom comes to the nest to **nurse** her kits.

Out of the Nest

Older kits hop around outside the nest.

They munch
on flowers
and grass.

Kits **shed** a lot of hair. They take time to fluff their fur.

Kits stand on their back legs when they are **curious**.

Sometimes they leap into the air. This joyful jump is called a binky!

Glossary

burrow—a hole or tunnel that an animal digs in the ground

curious—interested in learning more about something

litters—groups of babies born together

nurse—to feed babies milk

pets—animals that live with people

shed—to lose or let fall off

To Learn More

AT THE LIBRARY

Elora, Grace. *Bunnies.* New York, N.Y.:
Gareth Stevens Publishing, 2011.

Kalman, Bobbie. *Baby Bunnies.* New York,
N.Y.: Crabtree, 2010.

Wittrock, Jeni. *A Baby Rabbit Story.* Mankato,
Minn.: Capstone Press, 2012.

ON THE WEB

Learning more about
rabbits is as easy as 1, 2, 3.

1. Go to www.factsurfer.com.

2. Enter "rabbits" into the search box.

3. Click the "Surf" button and you will see a
   list of related Web sites.

With factsurfer.com, finding more information
is just a click away.

Index

The images in this book are reproduced through the courtesy of: Anneka, front cover; Martin Ruegner/ Age Fotostock, pp. 4-5; Shunyu Fan, pp. 6-7; Nick Biemans, pp. 8-9; Patricia Vazquez/ Glow Images, pp. 10-11; Juniors/ SuperStock, pp. 12-13, 18-19, 20-21; Juniors Bildarchiv/ Glow Images, pp. 14-15, 16-17.